SPOTTE

A GUIDE TO BRITISH RARE BREEDS

A fully illustrated Guide to British People, some who have become extinct,
others who are just about hanging on in quiet corners of this
green and pleasant land.

Gordon Thorburn and Paul Davies

This book is dedicated to
Andy Thorburn and Tom Davies
who were both proper coppers, and to
Gordon's daughters Frances and Katie
in fond memory of their father.

This was first published as "Some Missing Persons" in 2011
This re-named 'Spotted!' edition is published on Amazon 2023

The words here were written by my dear friend and
erstwhile work colleague from the 1970s when
we both had a brief career in advertising, his career in
the business lasting much longer than mine.

Gordon Thorburn was a copywriter then and later a writer of all sorts.
His 'Men and Sheds' book was a best seller,and he ghost wrote several more books.
We collaborated on one or two books this one being one our favourites.
He died in 2019 leaving me with this fine legacy: a book I love,
and words that I loved to illustrate. Some of the ideas within here came from him,
especially the ones about pubs as he was something of an expert on them.
Other ideas had their basis in stories and observations of mine which
he then weaved into something coherent.

All the people in here are based on people we have known or met.
The Schoolmaster is for instance based on Mr Trethewy, my old history teacher.
The Proper Copper is my own father, and the Rambler
has more than a passing resemblance to Gordon himself.
Way back when we were first friends and colleagues Gordon suggested that we might
walk the Pennine Way, backwards. By that he meant we start at the finish
and end at the start.We did most of it until his boots 'gave out'
and his feet could do no more, `so Rambler is very accurate.

So, it is my pleasure to introduce you to people who we do not
see very much these days and some who are almost extinct.
(there's no such thing as a bus conductor any more and if there were he or she `
would be called a Customer Relations Travel Consultant).
They are all here though: Rare Breeds, in every respect.
Originally called 'Some Missing Persons', I have taken the liberty of re-naming
this edition. Look out for them and if you spot one then make a note of it,
because these people are truly notable and worth celebrating.

Paul Davies
February 2023

www.pauldaviescartoons.com

WHO'S NEXT FOR EXTINCTION?

The types of people you saw every day only thirty years ago,
are going missing. Due to aggressive, often imported competitors, cultural
and material changes to habitats, shrinking feeding grounds and
breaks in the reproductive chain, their fate is sealed.
Some may continue to eke out a secret existence
in pathetically reduced circumstances.
Some may stoutly resist and rebel, but in vain.

PROPER DOCTOR

MAN WHO MENDS CARS

RAMBLER

BOOKSHOP OWNER

GOAT WOMAN

SCHOOLMASTER

NEWSPAPER SELLER

PUBS AND PUBLICANS

SCHOOLMASTER

BEST DRESSED MAN IN THE VILLAGE

HOUSEWIFE

ARTIST

BIKE WOMAN

BARBER

PROPER BARMAID

ROCKING BEECHNUTS

SCULPTOR

LESSER NATURAL RECEPTIONIST

TOURIST

PROPER COPPER

TRANSPORT CAFE OWNER

BANK MANAGER

SCHOOL COOK

14TH BARONET AND LADY

FARMER

SCHOOL MISTRESS

SPY

THE GHASTLY TRUTH AND WHOSE FAULT IS IT?

Our book describes those types of *homo sapiens*
which flourished in the Age of Common Sense,
when bottles of milk had cream on the top.
In those golden days, the term **Marketing** meant going daily to the butcher's,
the baker's and the greengrocer's;
Accountancy meant keeping the score; **Political Correctness** meant voting for the
Conservative Party; and **Technology** was a fountain pen
which didn't leak when you flew in a Vickers Viscount.

Since these four Forces of the Apocalypse have taken over,
the world has gone mad and the casualties have become unsustainable.
Indeed, you, gentle reader, may yourself belong to a threatened strand of humanity,
in this Age of Nonsense where inferior substitutes cost more
than the real thing and the Second Division is called the Championship.

So, please, brace up. You don't have to wear a baseball cap.
You need never get Digital VD. You can eat butter.
You can have funerals rather than Cremation and Interment Solutions.
But for how long? Alas and lack a day, it is already too late for some.

PROPER DOCTOR

Isolated examples may survive in remote parts of Scotland.

One of the strangest varieties of all, Proper Doctor only existed in one sex and did not have adolescent stages (*vide* Goat Woman). Proper Doctor simply appeared as an adult male aged 45 with his Gladstone bag already battered. In daylight, he would often wear plus-fours and a tweed jacket with leather elbow patches (*vide* Schoolmaster). If he came to see you at night, he would be dressed in black tie and dinner jacket.

      Proper Doctor's role was one of reassurance and confidence building. He was not familiar with the panoply of new drugs and tended to believe that illness should be carefully watched but allowed to run its course, with a little doctoral steering and an aspirin. He looked after his own health with Player's Navy Cut (ready rubbed) and regular doses of Highland Park, or Laphroig if he was feeling coldy.

      When he went to the shop in the morning for his newspaper, mints and matches, any locals in front of him would step aside deferentially. At the lodge and the golf club he was well liked and referred to as Doc.

      At the age of 65 he would retire to a country cottage, having rarely interfered drastically with anyone's life although he would have been greatly appreciated at the beginnings and the ends.

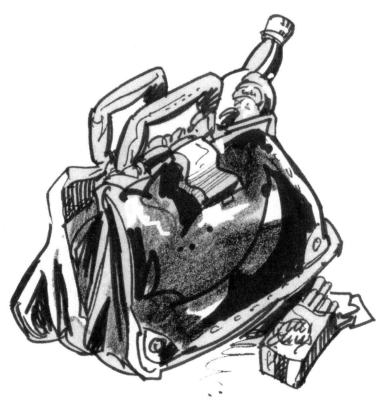

MAN WHO MENDS CARS

Sometime in the 1970s, a design engineer had the idea of putting a computer in a car. At that instant, an entire breed was sentenced to death and we can expect Man Who Mends Cars to be virtually extinct in the western world by about 2015AD. Then, there will remain only a few isolated individuals within whom will reside the last shreds of knowledge about how to repair cars rather than psychoanalyse them and reconstitute them with plug-in components.

By then, except in Famagusta and at Classic Car rallies, you will never see a Ford Cortina nor any kind of Austin, Morris, Triumph or Hillman. All old-style VW Beetles will have been squashed flat. No Citroen Deux Chevaux will be worth flogging. People will think the Fiat 500 is the Italian share index.

There will be no cars left without fuel-injected air-conditioned sports warranties and three-year ABS alloy airbags. Every car will bong at you to say that you have left the door open, the handbrake is on and you haven't fastened your belt yet. Equally newsworthily, every car will tell you that it's cold outside and there are roadworks on the M6. Every car will have more buttons on its radio/CD dooberry than were once considered necessary for the entire dashboards of twenty MG-TCs.

Meanwhile, Man Who Mends Cars looks out onto the road and sees a never changing stream of vehicles which are incomprehensibly complex inside and whose outsides cannot be told one from another. Eventually, the only task within his capabilities will be changing a tyre.

Today, if you want to spot Man Who Mends Cars, you will need to go to a small country town (non-commutable) or the back streets of a poor area of the city. Look for a rusty sign saying National Benzole or Pratt's Motor Spirit. There, inside a dark cavern with a rectangular hole in the floor, will be a stove burning sump waste. You will see some motor cycles (BSA C15, Ariel Square Four, Triumph Tiger Cub, Norton Dominator), the bonnet and wheels of a Riley Elf and several wiring harnesses on a hook. In the chaotic area designated 'office', there will be a picture of a Jowett Javelin, some horrible items to do with making tea, and a girlie calendar for 1972 provided by RW Grimbagg & Sons (Abrasives) Ltd.

The man himself, in a dark blue over-all, will be sitting on a bentwood chair eating a king prawn jalfraisi, part-payment for a job he did last year on the Taj Mahal owner's daughter's Mini Moke.

Related species and varieties:
MAN WHO HELPS MAN WHO MENDS CARS.

Several members of this migratory group attach themselves to each specimen of the main variety. They take it in turns to stand around watching while drinking tea.

RAMBLER

Will probably be extinct by 2025

Rambler's winter and summer coat is tweed, with check shirt, heather mixture stockings and stout boots. The male often has a deerstalker or a flat cap, the female a balaclava which rolls up to make a pom-pom hat. Both carry wooden walking sticks and small canvas rucksacks. You are very unlikely to spot any young.

Once especially common in Snowdonia and the Lake and Peak Districts and frequently sighted in other upland areas, Rambler could also be observed on a serviced campsite but sleeping in an ordinary two-man ridge tent.

Rambler is fast being driven out of habitat by invaders. Particularly ferocious competitors include Extreme Outdoor Leisure Pursuit Persons. They wear helmets designed by the same artist who draws giant ants for Walt Disney, and ride on a bicycle where Rambler was wont to walk. A kind of brightly coloured swimming costume promotes the smooth passage of air around their clearly visible contours. Their bicycles have two hundred gears and yet, curiously, are made to be carried as well as ridden.

Another invader, Healthy Wealthy Wide Boy, can best be described in a true story. Walking down from High Cup Nick in the north Pennines, your correspondent (a slovenly halfbreed sub-variety of Rambler) saw a strange being coming up. This being was wearing a black outfit. It was a type of shell suit made of a very advanced and glistening fibre which must have repelled water, wind, country smells and UV rays while keeping the wearer at a predetermined level of comfort. He also had black boots, a black rucksack, a black baseball cap and a black holster in which was secured his portable telephone. Not black was his aluminium, extensible Alpenstock thing with which, possibly, he meant to sound the depths of any obstructing stream.

Had he been asked the time, he would have revealed a wristlet watch carved from a pound of solid gold, made to resemble the instrument panel of a MIG 29 mounted in a souvenir cog wheel.

His plump son and heir wore an unco-ordinated ensemble of T-shirt, shorts, trainers and red baseball cap. Female consort, plump also, was similarly shirted and shorted but baht 'at. Her shiny white shoes had an ankle strap, a moderate heel and a painted big toe nail sticking out. Dangling on strings around her neck were whistle, compass and a map in a square, clear plastic doodah. What she proposed doing with any of these was not obvious.

In the face of such powerful forces Rambler, gentle and timid (timid, that is, except where blocked rights of way are concerned) can only retreat to the fireside nest, there to semi-hibernate beside a two-foot-high pile of Wainwrights.

BOOKSHOP OWNER

...occurs in both sexes. Driven out of populous areas by larger, more aggressive types, the remaining few Bookshop Owners survive in nooks and crannies.

Cyril Trumpet was the last scion of the family Trumpet, owners and runners of Trumpet & Son Publishing Bookshop since 1879. They hadn't published a book since the 'Trumpet's Care and Maintenance' series, marvellous little books brought out with brilliant timing in the 1960s and 70s. They told you everything you
needed to know about looking after mechanical typewriters, wooden tennis racquets, slide rules, comptometers, 78rpm records and washing machines with hand-operated wringers.

Cyril was a kindly soul with old-fashioned beliefs. He took an interest in all his customers and thought it his job to find what they wanted or, if he could not find it, to get it at whatever inconvenience to himself. He listened to what the publishers' sales reps said when they called to tell him about new books, and was available to meet them when he said he would be.

He looked at books for quality and originality and never allowed his own private views to interfere with his selections. So, even if he had been a bluestocking PC feminist manhater, he would still have had books in his shop with sexy pictures of females on the cover, if he thought they were good and would sell.

Similarly, even if Cyril had been a young gentleman graduate in 19th century Canadian Literature, with an MA in The Trials of Oscar Wilde and a deep bitterness at being a failed poet, he would still have been polite to anyone who came in his bookshop.

Cyril liked books because they are books. He liked good ideas and elegant style. He liked variety and thought that five different titles about quilting were quite enough, refusing to stock the other 128.

Unfortunately, Cyril could not work a computer and did not understand how the big stores could offer best-selling titles at a retail price lower than he had to pay wholesale. He did not understand The Market. He, foolishly, thought that the market was the people who had stalls on the square every Tuesday.

Poor Cyril. He sold his shop three years ago.
It's been Age Concern, Oxfam and British Heart Foundation.
Now it's going to be a pizza take-away.

GOAT WOMAN

Like Proper Doctor and Headmistress (*qv*), Goat Woman has no equivalent in the opposite sex and does not have an immature stage; she self-manifests aged 62 in a cottage or bungalow with a large field attached. Any future the type may have is dependent on the continued availability of such premises.

Normal appearance is in headscarf, Barbour and wellies although she may also be seen in woolly hat, man's tweed jacket, long tweed skirt and wellies.
Her calls are never, ever with the local accent; Goat Woman always talks County.

There are Solitary and Social varieties. The former lives entirely alone, feeding on lentils and goat dairy products. The latter can be spotted in the newsagent/tobacconist's and the betting shop before going to the pub. Here she lectures farmers on the relative virtues of the Toggenburg and the Golden Guernsey, and on herbal remedies for Pox, Scurf and Pink Eye. If people express the slightest interest, Goat Woman will enthusiastically enlighten them on the subtle differences in bouquet between billy goats of the Saanen and Anglo-Nubian breeds during the mating season.

Be careful. Elderly females wearing headscarf, Barbour, tweeds and wellies are not necessarily specimens of Goat Woman. They could be mere horse-persons, which are common enough, or Range Rover Hoorays which can be shot when there's an R in the month. If in doubt, listen for confirmation through tell-tale calls such as 'Saw the old Tog treading today. We were jolly well covered!' or 'Kid tried to pop out arse first, little bugger. Pushed him back in, turned him, and
Bob's your uncle!'

It is thought by scientists that Goat Woman is related to Dandy Dinmont Breeding Woman but this has not been proved in the laboratory.

NEWSPAPER SELLER

Any sightings should be reported to the Natural History Museum.

There are plenty of people who stand about selling papers but specimens of Newspaper Seller must, by definition, be recognisable in the dusk and rain by their cries alone. Saying 'Big Issue? Have a nice day' in a polite, self-effacing tone does not make one a Newspaper Seller, quite honestly.

The real thing was ever unmistakable. Anyone from north east Yorkshire would be able to infer from the distant cry of 'Baybay! Scabbay! Baybay!' that they were on the other side of the clearing from a man offering the paper, the Scarborough paper. That it was called the Evening News was a matter widely understood and so unnecessary to mention.

Strangers to the famous port 40 miles south would instantly realise that the man selling the late editions of the Hull Daily Mail was the one crying 'Hawdiwinnahs! Skinnywinnahs!' Like everybody else in Hull, with the possible exception of the specimen himself, they would never know the wherefore but would buy the paper anyway and without asking about the undernourishment of victorious horses.

In the Great Wen all those thousands of office mice, hurrying down their holes at the end of the day, used to lift their heads briefly at the familiar call of 'Tennerh! Ee-inn! Tennerh!' and, without looking at Newspaper Seller, drop a few coins into an outstretched hand in exchange for a copy of the Standard, the Evening Standard.

On Sundays, no members of the type were ever seen. Nobody knew where they went. Possibly they hibernated for the day, venturing forth only to the corner shop to purchase a copy of the Tie, Sunnay Tie, or possibly the Zerv Erah, or maybe the Noodawer-eh.

Scientists are still trying to prove that Working Men's Club and Institute Singing Man has evolved from Newspaper Seller, for some reason.

SIGNS OF OLD TIMES

Of all the unholy crimes committed by accountants and marketing executives, the decimation of our pubs and publicans is possibly the most odious.

A common-or-garden-as-muck Ye Olde Hayemayker Inne, one of 500 exactly similar managed houses serving smoothly flowing 'beer' at Arctic temperatures, plus Tyme Honoured Fayre cooked and frozen at the central kitchens, all served to the accompaniment of a repeating Kylie Minogue CD, is ideal. Everything can be controlled from head office. There are no variables.

One day, all pubs will be run by centrally trained managers.

There will be no more room for individuals.

THE SURLY OLD GIT

...is exactly as it was when its purpose in life was to cater for the eager, laughing crowds coming off shift from the drop forge. Now, hidden away on the canal bank, mid city, between the back of the Hospital for Tropical Diseases and the Yeung Chow Chow Fan Wholesale Warehouse, it has two sorts of customer:

regular and unwary.

The regulars, mostly journalists, are there in the hope of witnessing a Heritage Moment, when a stranger walks in and catches one of the last genuinely baleful glares left in the British leisure industry. The facial expression they are waiting for should have its own brown sign on the motorway. Infallibly, it is induced in the eponymous landlord by a new and insensitive customer's recitation of the following lines.

'Ah, mine host! A foaming pint of your finest draught mild, if you would be so kind. Very well then, I shall have bitter. Yes, the smooth will be fine. And a spritzer for my good lady here. Dry white wine and soda. Ah, right, well, a cider would be excellent. Or, indeed, as you say, a half of smooth. And what flavour crisps do we have this fine day?

Two packets of pork scratchings, of course.

Could you just top that pint up for me, please?'

THE KING'S BREECHES

This city-centre pub is very popular with exiles from the old Iron Curtain countries, since it reminds them so much of the railway-station waiting rooms back home. Connoisseurs of 1950s minimalism will also enjoy the five well-seasoned South American banknotes pinned to the stone-effect wallpaper above the bar.

Other establishments near-by offer a full menu plus blackboard specials, and live music in the evenings. The King's Breeches provides for a niche market to one side of the business-lunch crowd, with a small selection of superheated pies out of a Perspex cabinet. The free paper serviette assists easy eating rather than forcing on customers the embarrassing refinements of cutlery and plate. After dark, a juke box can be switched on by special request and any record played, provided it is *Crystal Chandeliers.*

Lecturers from the art college, attracted by the working-class atmosphere, drink no more than two units while chattering incessantly and waving their hands about. Journalists and flat-capped regulars prefer to ensure inner cleanliness with sequential pints of the memorable local bitter, reading their sporting papers in silence while flicking ash into dampening lagoons on the mahogany tops of original Victorian tables.

The tenant landlord, a dark taciturn man who is never rude to anyone but never friendly either, is greatly distressing the brewery by not dying. The predictions of the Chief Actuary of the Publicans, Sinners and General Insurance Co indicate that pub landlords' shortlivedness is second only to those who combine lion taming with drug dealing and cave diving, but our man is past 70 and showing no signs. When he does die, the brewery will rip the pub asunder, rename it The Tup and Tart, install satellite TV, a juke box, and a manager who will have to call the police on Fridays and Saturdays.

THE SUV AND HALF

This ancient wayside inn is handy for the farmers round about but they prefer to go the extra two miles into town to The Mended Bucket. The local fuzz apply the breathaliser enthusiastically so people from town don't come here either. Plenty of space is thus assured for holidaymakers and their children from the caravan site, operating their Playstations and spreading their Lego across the single bar-room that used to be public, saloon and snug.

On Sunday lunchtimes, one end of the bar is reserved for the local government officials, journalists and call-centre managers from the neo-Classical flagpoled estate where Low Rutter Farm used to be. They discuss motor cars and personal computers, with lawn mowers and pond linings occasionally allowed as guest subjects.

At The SUV and Half, food is served strictly 12 noon-2pm and 6pm-9pm. The menu offers a wide range of international exotica: moussaka, curry, chile con carne, sweet and sour pork. Home-made steak and kidney pie is a small, ping-able oval dish filled with dark brown fluid in which lurk a few lumps of bovine gristle. On top of the dish, but not attached to it, is a pale beige, oval object about six inches high and only fractionally heavier than air, which looks like something growing on a fallen trunk in ancient woodland.

The electric, flickering, pretend-candle wall lights cause migraines while illuminating the pair of plastic duelling pistols and the brass coal scuttles filled with pampas grass. The attractive female bar staff will leave their private conversations and text messaging if asked. On a cork notice board are colour postcards also showing attractive females but nude and kneeling in the sea.

The landlord, originally a car salesman from Basildon, spends a great deal of money at the hairdresser's and affects a nice line in gold necklaces, medallions and bangles. As you can easily observe, he has a hairy chest. He normally wears white leather slip-on shoes but also has a fawn pair. Soon he will sell to Snuggle Inns. This nationwide chain will build an extension of Spartan bedrooms and open a restaurant offering (see above).

YE OLDE SUNNE DRYED TOMATOE

Visitors to this remote and historic ex-hostelry, far up in the hills where rivers rise, always used to enjoy looking at the old photographs on the wall. These reflected a bygone age when the local produce show was held here, customers formed football and darts teams and turned up in Toyota pick-ups.

Those were the days, my friends, when the pub was the social *sine qua non* of a scattered rural community. The community is still scattered but if anybody wants a pint now it has to be a widget tin from the supermarket down the valley; no pints have been sold at Ye Tomatoe for a twelvemonth.

Yes, in that short time Signor Pomodoro Lambretta, front of house, and Darren 'Sharon' Maclaren, chef, transformed the place. Before, you could only get bitter, lager, Guinness and two sorts of sandwich: cheese and pickle, or cheese. Under Pommy and Sharon, you could have Saltimbocca Siciliano, Fegato alla Milanese, Pavarotti alla Mariolanza and various fusion dishes, including Szechuan Ostrich Stroganoff and Thai Broken Harbour Soup with Wild Orkney Octopus. You washed these down with 35 different sorts of Bardolino and 27 of Frascati. If you got too merry you could have bed and full Italian breakfast for the price of a farm labourer's week's wages.

It was not long before the two proprietors discovered that Upper Weirdale was no place for a gastropub. Their loan was called in and they had to sell the place as a private house, so that was that.

THE JACK THE RIPPER

Theme Pubs appear and disappear with equal suddenness, like flowers in the desert. Not long ago there were no such things as theme pubs and soon there will be no such thing again. They therefore offer a rare opportunity to observe a species from the very beginnings of existence to extinction.

A modern, redbrick pub on the new side of town used to be The Slow Worm and Pikelet and, before that, The White Hart. All traces of previous lives have disappeared in its reincarnation as the haunt of the famous stomach slitter.

The main room, the Whitechapel 1888 Lounge, features contemporary theatre bills and taped music of the kind which the pub chain's marketing manager imagines was heard in Victorian East End music halls. So, to the strains of *Get me to the church on time* and *Chas & Dave's Greatest Hits*, female bar staff, mostly resting actresses, strut about dressed as 19th century prostitutes with appropriate boils, scabs, suppurating sores, missing teeth etc. They approach male customers with a sassy walk, hand on hip and a toss of the head, saying 'Fancy a nice pint, dearie?'

When it's time for a barmaid's break a male member of staff, dressed in black cloak and top hat, will spread artificial blood all over while acting as if slicing her neck with an open razor. He'll then drag her off, calling after him 'Clear that up, will you?'

In the Annie Chapman Bar, customers can don virtual-reality headsets and re-enact the ripping in question, selecting one of three roles: the horrid slasher, someone looking through the window or, of course, they can experience the last moments of Ms Chapman herself.

The Long Lizzie Stride Bar is done out like an old mortuary with waxwork naked bodies lying on marble slabs in various stages *post mortem*. When customers tire of the near-freezing temperature they can wander into the toasty warmth of the Catherine Eddowes Eaterama, where steaming hot joints of the day are offered in a do-it-yourself carvery.

If you do fancy a nice pint, you have a choice of three micro-brewery real ales: Marie Kelly Koff-Kure (ABV 5.8), Polly Nicholls Jugular Jangler (ABV 6.4) and Liza Pearl Pulmonary Drain (ABV 8.2).

The manager, upstairs with his CCTV screens and instant computerised till read-outs and stock-level displays, will shortly move to HQ. There will be a big meeting at which the marketing and finance people will discuss the next retheming, possibly to Imperial Rome, Seaside Holidays, the War of Jenkins' Ear, Pre-Raphaelite Painters, Mary Queen of Scots or Birds of Prey. After a while even they will realise that the theme pub is one of the silliest notions anyone ever thought of.

SCHOOLMASTER

Extinction is inevitable if it hasn't happened already. We're talking state school here; all sorts of rare types thrive in the private sector.

Schoolmaster wore a suit to work or, at the very least, a sports jacket with leather elbow patches (*vide* Proper Doctor). He smoked a pipe which he fuelled with WD&HO Wills' Gold Block and could often be seen, winter and summer alike, drawing on his pipe while cycling along on his Rudge sit-up-and-beg. In atrocious weather, his wife drove him to school in the family Ford Popular.

At work, he wore a university gown which had long tears in it and was covered with chalk dust. He strode along the corridor with purposeful mien as knots of children unravelled before him. He could remember the names (surnames, naturally) of all the children he ever taught and they, for the whole of their lives, remembered him fondly, gratefully and distinctively. They remembered what he taught them, too.

Schoolmaster is not to be confused with Schoolteacher. Schoolteacher smokes dope, listens to Leonard Cohen records, supports Manchester United and wears trainers and jeans to work. Although both varieties, one now so rare and one so common, always shared a certain naiveté about life in the big wide world, Schoolmaster's was of an innocent, forgivable sort.

He knew all there was to be knowed about the A-level physics, Maths, English or History syllabus and nothing at all about life, or anything else except the clues in The Guardian crossword. He realised this and confined his advice to his recognised areas of expertise.

Schoolteacher, similarly specialised, nevertheless carries banners in demos, feels solidarity with the miners but not the farmers and has fierce arguments about the Brexit, the wars in Ndanga, Irdukhistan and the Undisputed Territories, and believes equally in a woman's right to choose an abortion and a child's right to choose what it learns at school.

As far as scientific research has been able to show, there have been no young Schoolmasters leaving the university for forty or more years.

BEST DRESSED MAN IN THE VILLAGE

A vacancy has arisen in the post of Honorary Village Figurehead, Titlingham St Margaret. Would suit retired major, colonel or wing commander with wife extant. Applicants must be prepared to chair Parish Council, school governors, et cetera.

Naval officers tended to retire on the coast, so the villagers of Titlingham, deep in the heart of Suffolk, always expected a senior soldier or airforce chap to come and lead them in their battles against the swirling tides of progress, and they were not disappointed.

The wife (extant), who was called Susan or Verity, also did chairing, of the village fete committee and the WI, and organised the flower rota in the church. She bought all her provisions at the village shop apart from, obviously, a few things that had to be sent from Fortnums.

He, known universally as The Major or, at a pinch, The Squadron Leader, drank halves of best, with a handle, three times a week at the pub. He'd hob-nob indiscriminately with the vicar, the poacher, the gamekeeper, the butcher, the horse dealer, the doctor (qv), the goat woman (also qv), the gardener up at the house and the mechanic who looked after his old Wolseley. He'd never tell secrets to the village policeman, not that the village policeman would want to know anyway.

The Major, you see, was not the squire or the lord of the manor. The Major was of the village. He was *primus inter pares* and most definitely *primus*, but he clipped his own hedge, grew his own roses, and called all the men (except the vicar and the doctor) by their first names, likewise the daughters thereof. He doffed his hat to the ladies and never smoked his pipe at the nativity play. His shoes (brown Oxford brogues with leather soles, hand made) were always polished to a mirror sheen. He generally wore one of his collection of six three-piece Savile Row tweed suits but could also be sighted on sunny afternoons, walking his two spaniels, in crimson or mustard cord trousers and cashmere cardigan.

He's gone now. Defeated. Half the village is weekenders and commuters. In any case, retired officers these days don't keep their ranks as titles and move to the country. Many of them didn't even go to public school. Unable to retire gracefully, they write books, join security firms or become pop stars.

The poacher's gone too. Can't afford the house prices. A merchant banker, retired at 45, bought the old rectory the major used to live in and planted Leylandii all around it. The shop has shut, the pub is a restaurant with bar, and the school is struggling for numbers. A doctor from town holds a weekly surgery in the village hall and nobody has seen a policeman for months.

It's sad, really. Very sad.

HOUSEWIFE

There are very few young of the species Housewife and even fewer surviving to the adult stage. Extinction is near.

There used to be a great many books written about the habitat and seasonal behaviour of Housewife, for instance *Every Woman's Book of Home Making* published in the 1930s which states 'A large proportion of the Housewife's time is occupied in planning, buying and preparing food, and indeed this is one of her biggest responsibilities. If, through lack of knowledge, the Housewife does not provide body building foods, then the children will be rickety and stunted.' It also says 'Many people spend too much money on jam, sugar and sweets', and 'Friday. The Living Room. Take up carpets and rugs, place heavy furniture in centre of room and cover with dust sheets. Clean ceiling and walls and wash all paintwork. Wash all china, glass and other ornaments. Beat all rugs and mats out in the open.'

No such books are written now except to present aspects of Housewife's activities as pastimes, leisure crafts, ways to self empowerment or, in acute cases, the new rock and roll. Cookery books are especially popular although many of their purchasers rarely cook anything, despite having kitchens with the finest professional equipment in battleship-quality stainless steel, built-in satellite microwaves, Art Nouveau chandeliers and dangling bunches of herbs. What they don't have is the ability to follow written cooking instructions.

Take 'Oyster Relish' from *A Plain Cookery Book for the Working Classes* by Charles Elme Francatelli, once Chief Cook to Queen Victoria. This little book was published in 1852 but it still made perfect sense in 1952 and, to Housewife, perfect sense now.

'Put the oysters, with their liquor and a little water or milk, into a saucepan; add a bit of butter kneaded, that is, well mixed with a table-spoonful of flour; pepper and a little salt; stir the oysters over the fire until they have gently boiled for about five minutes, and then pour them into a dish containing some slices of toasted bread. Strew all over their surface equal quantities of bread raspings and grated cheese; hold a red-hot shovel over the top until it becomes slightly coloured and eat this little delicacy hot.'

What of today's non-Housewife reading this? A *bit* of butter? How many oysters? How many bread raspings? What's a rasping? Have we got a shovel, darling? When the shovel becomes slightly coloured, what colour should it be?

Tea served in a cup & saucer.

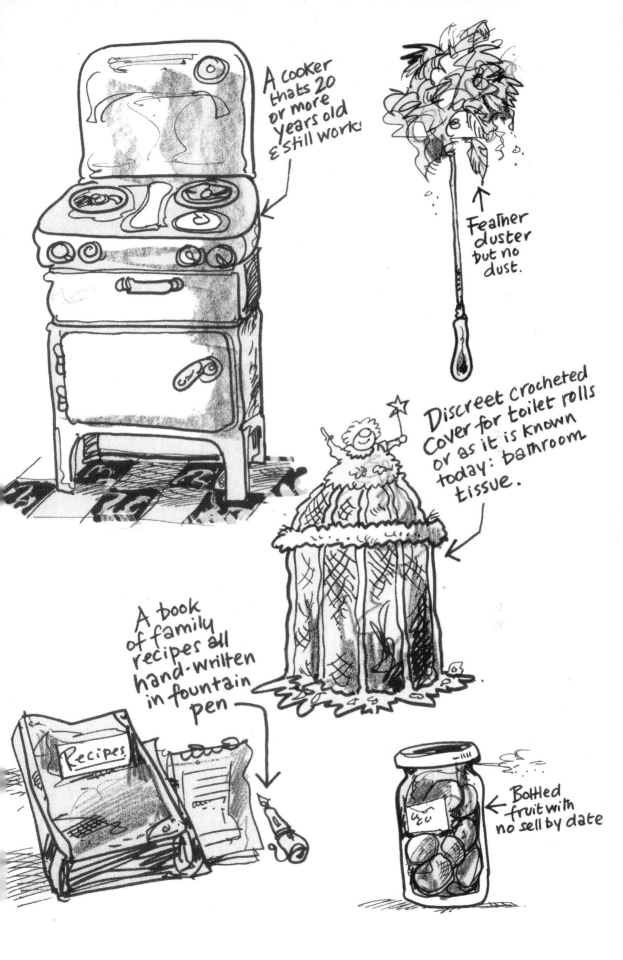

A cooker thats 20 or more years old & still works

Feather duster but no dust.

Discreet Crocheted Cover for toilet rolls or as it is known today: bathroom tissue.

A book of family recipes all hand-written in fountain pen

Recipes

Bottled fruit with no sell by date

ARTIST

Evolution has produced a more belligerent species, Conceptual Artist (Con Artist for short), whose young have pretty well eliminated Artist, the dignified predecessor, from natural habitats like boozers and brothels.

Although still distinguished from Con Artist by the ability to paint and draw, Artist has become shy, reclusive and largely nocturnal, and so is rather difficult to spot among all the other drunks, neurotics and sex maniacs.

Gone are the days when the least attentive naturalist could hardly fail to stumble across the telltale signs of Artist: paint, brushes, canvas, nude models, charcoal and empty beer crates. That has all disappeared because Artist's only survival strategy, the talent for depiction, has become almost irrelevant.

As with so many other endangered animals, here we have a complete failure to adapt to changing circumstances. While Artist continues to attempt to emulate or surpass previous artistic achievements, Con Artist has realised that there is no point in trying to paint something better than, say, *The Odalisque*, when you can video a beautious naked female sitting on the toilet. This is doubly effective because, when you get tired of looking at the woman on the bog, you can record an episode of *The Simpsons* over the top of it.

Con Artist may have no obvious ability and may look like any other pasty-faced, body-piercing degenerate but the hypnotic call makes him/her more successful at grabbing whatever money there is knocking about.

Thus, Con Artist will easily persuade a squillionaire or a borough council to give a massive grant so a room can be filled with chicken noodle soup. Indeed, the hypnosis lasts so long that the same source will happily pay again next season for Con Artist's *Cabinet maker's mother knits a dining table in purple and yellow wool*.

The much less assertive Artist, pleading weakly for money to buy some paint to do a picture of Exmoor at sunset, will find there is nothing left in the kitty. Even if there were, Artist wouldn't get any. After all, nobody has thought it worthwhile to knit a table before, whereas loads of Artist specimens have painted landscapes and thousands and thousands of people have pictures hanging in rooms which, more creatively, could be filled with soup.

BIKE WOMAN

Survival depends on the continued existence of huge motor cycles.

In the spurious world of advertising, Bike Woman is a slinky young blonde beauty with nothing on beneath her leather jacket, which is otherwise well filled and unzipped to thewaist She sits astride a bike as if she and it were lust incarnate.

In reality, Bike Woman can be large, mature and frightening of aspect, to be approached with caution. She always has a male consort whose uses include driving the bike, refuelling the bike, polishing thebike, having an off-putting appearance, and mating. Places to spot Bike Woman include those favoured by the male consorts for summer rutting displays, such as the Isle of Man, the Hartside cafe between Penrith and Alston, and the Cat and Fiddle pub between Macclesfield and Buxton.

Your correspondent once saw a fine specimen of Bike Woman wearing a uniquely low-cut leather jacket, clearly custom tailored to show off the pushed-up breasts which were completely covered in squirly tattoos. A quick glance had to be sufficient, since the look received from Bike Woman unmistakably indicated that certain people were not the type for which the exhibits were designed. Since the consort was even taller and more muscular, there could be no argument. Your correspondent was walking past a bookshop window at the time and his averted gaze fell on a display copy of the Complete Guide to British Decorated Jugs.

Bike Woman is closely related to several other species, none of them common but all hoping to escape extinction. These are All-in Mud Wrestling Woman, Second-hand Furniture Woman (House clearance's a speciality), and Rough Pub Owning Woman.

BARBER

Still found in gentlemen's clubs and those seaside resorts popular with the retiring middle classes.

Because Barber's shop used to be a men-only place it was the main retail outlet for the London Rubber Company, whose population-preventing products were known as 'Something for the weekend, sir?'. Even when Boots the Chemist decided to overturn its founder's ruling and sell these symbols of decadence and sin, for years most chaps on a promise would still rather buy them from Barber, a fellow man, than from a rosy-cheeked Boots Saturday girl or a fierce-looking lady pharmacist. Of course, this was in the days before condoms for £1 in pub toilets, before they had more flavours than an American ice-cream parlour, and before the sexual revolution (*circa* 1965) when the proposal to install a contraceptive vending machine in the students' union at Leeds University was front page news in the Daily Mirror.

Youths of that era and before, hoping that tonight would be the night, had to seek the red and white striped pole to obtain the necessary supplies. Such a boy went into the shop, all fragile brashness, and said something quietly to Barber who was busy cutting another's hair. 'Sorry, son' said Barber loudly. 'We only do them in packets of three.'

Ah well, the swinging, up-and-down adjustable leather chairs are gone and the glass cabinet no longer contains brilliantine, macassar oil and packets of Blue Gillette. The indicative sound is no longer the snip-snip of super-sharp scissors or the fine scrape of the cut-throat razor slipping through the foam, because an entirely new, loud and abrasive noise has taken over, made by something you would never, ever have seen in any proper Barber's shop, not ever, ever, ever: a hairdrier.

SUB-VARIETIES

Hairless Shortback, often visually impaired, can only do one style of haircut although he asks you how you would like it cut (answer: in complete silence).

Flowery Limpwrist is a newish variety which may outlast the others. He cannot do any style of haircut at all but takes endless trouble and vast quantities of your time to wash, cut, blow-dry, primp and spray your hair until you look like Best of Breed at the sheep show.

Sylvia Uniform wears smartly pressed trousers (possibly pin-striped), a crisp white shirt and the kind of black tie favoured by saloon card-sharps in Western films. She deals with her male customers in the same way that a fishmonger deals with a haddock. She may levy fines for smartphone interruptions. Quid pro quo for the paying male victim is the luxurious maternal depth of cushioning bosom at certain points in the procedure.

PROPER BARMAID

In the days when keg bitter and draught lager were making their first unholy inroads into the sacred temples of real ale, someone wrote a fine poem:

> Not turning taps
> But pulling pumps
> Gives barmaids ample
> Breasts and rumps.

In these few words lay hidden the deep, agonising dread which the increasing popularity of pasteurised beer and lager brought about in the drinking man of that time. If it were no longer necessary to be versed in the arts of keeping and drawing live beer and holding one's own in the superior forms of repartee induced by real ale, then anybody could be a barmaid. You'd get college girls, or hitch-hikers from New Zealand. Anybody. If barmaiding ceased to be a skilled trade and became a mere function, the end of the world was nigh.

Sadly, it's all come true. Bar staff these days are invariably university graduates and/or from the Colonies or central Europe. Roughly half of all pints sold are lager and many of the rest are the sterilised, homogenised, filtered, denatured, supercooled, smoothly flowing ersatz caricature of beer which the brewers have foisted on us, not because we asked for it but because they wanted to de-skill the brewing, carting, storing and serving process.

Soulless marketing managers and accountants, by replacing proper beer with counterfeit trash, not only made their deplorable mark on the British public house. They also consigned the Proper Barmaid to oblivion.

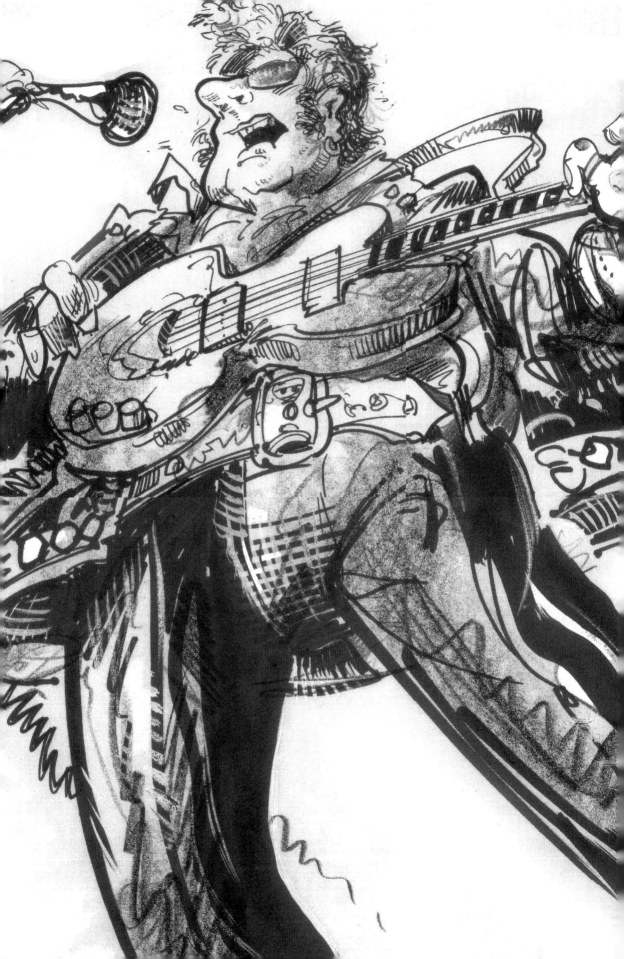

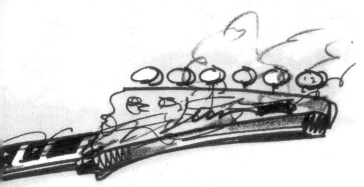

VIC SHINDIG AND THE ROCKING BEECHNUTS

Vic came to prominence in 1963 as Victor Bradshaw, in the village hall at
Stonkington Parva. With three classmates from the town grammar school he
formed The Binder Twines, a folk/blues group which broke up after an
argument over the relative merits of Turnip Patch Joe, Blind Lemon
Jefferson, and Peter, Paul and Mary.

Vic formed a rock and roll band and learned the complete works of Chuck
Berry, Buddy Holly, Eddie Cochran, Ray Charles and Jerry Lee Lewis, plus all the
new Beatles and Stones numbers as they came along.

Failing to be booked at anywhere bigger than the Conservative Working Men's Club,
the Rocking Beechnuts disbanded after ten fabulous years together. Family life, mortgages
and package holidays filled two more decades for Vic until, in
1998, redundant and divorced, he decided to re-form the band.

The original drummer was in prison in Saudi, the bass player was Supply
Chain Solutions Vice President, Northern Hemisphere, of an American fast-
food chain, and the rhythm guitar was running a lap-dancing club in
Thailand. Undaunted, Vic went around the pubs. He soon collected his musicians:
highly competent, devoted to Chuck Berry and able to play after ten pints.

Vic Shindig is performing at village halls again, with his Rocking Beechnuts.
Goodness gracious, great jolly B goods, they are the cure for the summertime blues. They're
going to tell you how it's going to be but, when they're sixty four, this could be the last time.

Scientists claim to have identified a sub-variety,
Big Mouth Disco. Usually booked for mixed-age parties and supper dances because of the
low cost, BMD is in fact a kind of Vic Shindig *alter ego*, in that he clears dance floors rather
than fills them. He insists on playing The Birdie Song and Hi Ho Silver Lining at every gig,
and forces arthritic pensioners to do the Dashing White Sergeant.

SCULPTOR

Name ten famous sculptors. *Er, right, er, Henry Moore, Rodin, er, Michelangelo, er, whatsername, Audrey Hepburn was it, Epstein, there you are, he's one, and that chap who did the discus thrower, and who was it did the goddess with her arms fallen off...?*

Name one sculptor working today. *Er, what do you call that woman with the plaster of Paris house?* No, no, no, she's not Sculptor. She's...well, anyway. *What about the Angel of the North?* Yes, quite.

Regular readers of *The Mallet* (incorporating *Chisellers' Monthly*) and *The Marble Importers' Index* will know a few living examples but, for most people, sculpture is some weird writhing metal things stuck on the end of the new council offices.

So, sculptor survives, and that despite the habit which poultry keepers call 'laying out', that is, nesting everywhere except in the home nesting box. Readers may remember seeing female Sculptor in the pub with her hair and her over-alls covered in white dust, asking the beefier men if they'd model for her. You don't see her now because she's transmogrified into Installation Artist and has been paid millions of sponduliks for her latest oeuvre, but the distinctive nesting-box behaviour remains the same.

The oeuvre in question, called 'Marsupialness' consists of ten beefy redundant coal miners dressed only in Armani sunglasses, hand-made hairnets of bright blue nylon sea-fishing line, and very loose-fitting Harris tweed plus fours. The left legs of their trousers are filled variously and severally with custard powder, parsnip seeds, Shap granite chips and those bits of polystyrene packaging which fly all over the place. Visitors are invited to feel inside the trousers and transfer the contents of a left leg into a right leg, having first waited in an orderly queue.

There is no room in this scenario for the male of Sculptor so he must, as always, be consoled by other species which may be attracted perhaps by his eccentricity and long hair. These miscellaneous females allow male Sculptor to wrap their bare breasts in plaster bandages. From the moulds thus produced he casts fibreglass replicas of their bosoms, which make for a novel trophy display in the hall.

LESSER NATURAL RECEPTIONIST

The seedy yet enchanting market-square hotel has been almost entirely swallowed up and made hostile by the big hotel groups. Except in certain rural parts of Ireland, you will never now see: *Lunch Menu   Soup or Melon   Steak and Kidney Pie or Poached Haddock   Ice cream or jelly* ...served by an elderly waitress wearing a black dress with white, lace trimmed apron and cap while, in the bar, farmers with their boots on lament the price of fat lambs.

As the hotel chains have devastated the environment, so the Common Centrally Trained Receptionist, with her gleaming smile and mechanical charm has more or less obliterated her more tender relative. The Common Receptionist's calls, for example "Would you just like to register for me?", "Would you just like to sign here for me?" and "Good morning thank you for calling the Royal Halfmast Heritage White Swan Hotel Wagglethorpe Tanya speaking how may I help you?", are widely heard today across the land.

If you are lucky and chance upon one of the few remaining specimens of the Lesser Natural, the call can be completely unpredictable, for example "Hello, yes, isn't it awful? Oh no, I don't think we have a reservation in that name, who did you speak to?"

You may witness this in a country hotel which, having been recently refurbished, has all the pretensions of the Royal Halfmast Heritage chain but, being independently owned, has no access to head office. Despite having pink tasselled lampshades everywhere and a menu card big enough to have propelled the Cutty Sark, it has no choice but to employ a Lesser Natural Receptionist. In which case, an incident like the following may ensue.

Man on room phone: Hello, there's something wrong with my bath.
LNR: Oh, I am sorry. What's the matter?
Man: The water is running out. It won't fill even with the taps full on.
LNR: Oh, yes, I see. I'll get on the phone straight away for a plumber.
Man: No need, my dear. Just find a plug and send it up.

Scientists have suggested that Natural Receptionist (Doctor's) is a related species and they may be right. She treats incoming patients on the assumption that they are malingering imbeciles and components of a secret plot to discredit the adored doctor in many unspecified ways, and are intent on carrying off said Receptionist for sale into the white slave trade.

TOURIST

Why do we have a TOURIST industry, why do we have national and regional TOURIST boards, why does every town from Thurso to Ramsgate, from Middlesbrough to Haverfordwest, encourage TOURISTS with a TOURIST Information Centre, when nobody will admit to being one?

Oh no, we're not a Tourist. We're a traveller. Tourist is a herding or flocking species, like the lemming or the hartebeest, the starling or the sheep. Like the honey bee, Tourist behaves predictably according to genetically implanted patterns.

Traveller is the solitary bee, the imaginative individual who discovers new lands and enjoys their quaint attributes before the blindly destructive droves of Tourist come along and trample the flowers.

This is an odd distinction to make, because 'traveller' is generally taken to mean one with hippy and herbal tendencies, who camps in a bender in somebody's field until forced to relocate using an ancient blue Ford Transit. Or, it's one with tinkering tendencies (*vide* Gypsy) who follows an annual circuit in his caravan. Or, a traveller is one who drives a saloon car very fast each day between one bed-and-breakfast hotel on a city's outskirts and another, stopping in between to take orders for industrial disinfectant.

A tourist, however, is "one who travels for pleasure or culture, visiting a number of places for their objects of interest, scenery, or the like" (Shorter Oxford). So the earthbound migratory species Holidaymaker evolved into the flying species Tourist, which went into denial and emerged as Traveller. Travellers now are two a penny but Tourists are much harder to spot in the UK although they winter plentifully in the USA and Japan.

PROPER COPPER

The sergeant on night duty at the police station picked up the telephone. One of his PCs had, very reluctantly, arrested a man as drunk and disorderly. This man had been doing no real harm, merely insisting that his name was Alma Cogan and promising that he would stop singing 'Sugarbush I love you so' as soon as a policeman had kissed him goodnight.

The sergeant knew that the regular police doctor was on holiday so he called in the locum, who duly arrived. On the floor of the Interview Room, as in all police stations throughout the land, there was a white line. One of the tests for drunkenness in those pre-breathaliser days was for the subject to walk down the line, one foot placed directly in front of the other in the manner of a fashion model on a tightrope.

The locum doctor looked at the arrested man, and smiled at the sergeant. The sergeant divined that here was a medic who had not done this job before.

"White line test, sir" said the sergeant, pointing to the line.

"Yes, of course" said the doctor, intelligently grasping what was required. With that completed, the doc made a few notes and tried to look competent.

"Pin test, sir" said the sergeant, extracting a dressmaker's pin kept for this very purpose in his uniform jacket lapel.

The standard method of conducting the pin test had always been to drop the pin on the floor, not to check the relative quietness of the interview room but to watch the subject trying to pick it up. This doctor had a new way. He stuck the pin in the back of the man's neck. At the resulting yelp, he wrote in his notes 'Reactions Normal'.

Most people's idea of Proper Copper is a Dixon of Dock Green, firm but fair, clipping urchins around the ear and telling mischief makers to get along home with you. With the greatest respect to Jack Warner, Dixon was only part of the whole being. In the programme, he never displayed the essential humour of Proper Copper, especially of the practical-joking kind, as did another night-shift sergeant who knew there was to be an exhumation in the churchyard next morning, at dawn as per usual practice. He told the probationary constable to keep a special eye on the churchyard at first light as there had been a spate of body-snatchings.

In the days when the police knew who people were and talked to them, a PC was given some gossip in the post office about a group of hairy squatters who had moved in on a certain little old lady. Apparently, they were making life a misery for her.

To quote from the PC's subsequent report: "I gained entry through a window which had fortunately been broken by a stone thrown up from a passing car. I attended while the squatters left at the lady's request".

TRANSPORT CAFE OWNER

May have been saved from extinction by reductions in the motorway building programme.

A transport cafe on the A5 near Cannock used to serve 'The Lot' at four shillings; nobody ever finished it. Famous places, like Tony's Caff on the A1, now a massive estate of filling stations and fast-food 'outlets', are sadly missed.

In the few transport cafes remaining, you will rarely see anyone who is not driving a lorry, where you used to get everything in the car park from a Rolls Royce to a tandem. People went because the food was massively plentiful, very tasty, slightly decadent, extraordinary good value, and accompanied by a pint mug of tea. You permed your order from a long, long list of ingredients on the wall, got your tea, your knife and fork and a raffle ticket, and went and sat down until a woman in a flowery pinny came in with a steaming plateful shouting "Eighty three!".

Nowadays, the staff are the only women in the place. The customers are men in over-alls who resent the poor food and high prices of the motorway services and hate Little Chefs which only allow cars, not that they would go in anyway. You can't blame these professionals if they feel civilians should go to their own oases and leave transport cafes to the transport.

Scientists have identified two sub-varieties of Transport Cafe Owner so far. Eel and Pie Shop Owner occurs exclusively in the urban south-east of England. Distinguishing behaviour includes the offer of some hot green water with the pie, accompanied by the call 'Wan parsley gravy, me old china?' or 'Wan liquor, me old cock sparrer?'

Oatcake Shop Owner occurs in Staffordshire and is active only in the mornings.

Operators in lay-by caravans, old buses etc do not countsince they employ no women in pinnies, have a restricted menu, and can relocate to a new habitat at any season, eg Sunday market or steam rally.

BANK MANAGER

The letter was from the Wold Newton and Yangtze Kiang Ship Canal Penny Bank, signed by Nicci Gristhorpe, Valued Client Liaison Supervisor (Non Internet). It said:

> *We are delighted to offer you, Valued Client, our new Platinum Card plus Gold Cards for all your relatives (minimum age two years), and a personal loan facility of £50,000 for any purpose. Projects thus funded for other Valued Clients recently have included a wasp farm, the restoration of a complete set of four early Victorian wooden legs, and an armed uprising in the Dutch Antilles. Call your Personal Banker today.*
>
> *Meanwhile, let me take this opportunity of informing you of our restructured range of Valued Client Service Furnishments. Overdrafts - 2% above base rate, compounded daily. Writing letters to offer overdrafts - £50. Responding to requests for overdrafts - £50. Confirming overdrafts by letter - £50. Writing letters to apologise for one of our Habitual Patron Prudence Deliberators mentioning your overdraft in public in a loud voice - £50. Additional charges - £25. Supplementary charges - £12.50. Other maintenance and referral charges - £50.*

With the letter scrunched up in his hand, the recipient set off for his branch, expecting to see his bank manager and old friend, Mr Hubert Duvet. Imagine his chagrin when he was greeted, not by Duvet of the black jacket and striped trousers but by a forceful young woman in clunky shoes, a short-skirted pale blue suit and a tight, white, low cut T-shirt. She said "Welcome to the WNYKSCPB? I am your Personal Banker? And you are?"

"I want to see Duvet!" he cried. "He knows who I am. See, that's my name, on my leather Wold Newton cheque book cover that they gave me thirty years ago, there, in gold blocking, Godfrey Horsforth."

"Godfrey, Mr Duvet has gone?" said the young woman, not noting the wince her familiarity engendered. "He's taken early retirement? We are the masters now?"

She showed him to a chair and sat at her desk in the middle of the mauve-carpeted open plan arrangement which had replaced the oak-doored offices since his last visit. "I'd like to explain our continuous review policy of service improvement?" said the WNYKSCPB/PB. "We are making a number of positive pre-adjustments to secondary fiscalate inputs on an on-going basis in order to ensure maximum capability of meeting customer needs?"

Mr Horsforth stood, went to the counter and made arrangements to transfer his all to the Filey Fishermen's Friendly Society.

It is probable, scientists believe, that a variety of Bank Manager was Small Provincial Town Stockbroker, distinguishing mark being the surname followed by '& Co' engraved on the office window. Owing to extinction, this belief is now impossible to prove either way.

SCHOOL COOK

Wandering near a school you will see, beside the litter bin, scores of garishly coloured empty foil packets and plastic bottles. These high-tech indestructibles were made to contain worthless rubbish. The bottles had coloured sugar water. The packets, made ten times bigger than necessary, held a few imitation witchetty grubs made of starch and glue and deep-fried air.

Just as the aggressive grey squirrel displaced the meeker red, so the Worthless Rubbish Industry displaced School Cook. County councils used to allow School Cook to buy her own raw materials. She did deals with farmers, gardeners and parents. Dinners of surpassing excellence, made from fresh, local ingredients, came out of her primitive kitchens. This would not do, naturally, so School Cook was regulated, centralised, provided with microwave ovens and frozen chips thereto and told to keep the vending machines stocked.

Today's children, you see, are completely different to yesterday's and require a totally new approach. Sociologists have shown that school dinners are fundamentally flawed. They are, in fact, dehumanising. The school dinner, as such, parallels the food-event hierarchy of the works canteen, which ultimately derives from the master-servant, castle-and-gate structure inherent within the holy communion system of the established church.

We should refocus in terms of à la carte meal solutions, allowing customers to make information-based decisions while gaining real-time experience in listing-tool technology. After completing a risk assessment, customers may elect to bring in their own food. Trained staff with health and safety certificates will handle the hot pans and do any stirring, slicing and other dangerous or physical work...

A group of children aged between five and eleven is gathered around a cast-iron stove in a whitewashed-brick classroom. It is snowing outside. Inside, the children are waiting for the stove to melt their vitamin-rich, full cream school milk, a third of a pint of which is issued to each child every day in a returnable, understated glass bottle. The boys are all in grey or brown shirts, home-knitted Fair Isle pullovers, grey flannel shorts, grey stockings and black boots. The girls are all in pleated grey, brown or navy blue skirts, home-knitted cardigans, white shirts, white stockings and stout shoes. No-one has ever eaten artificially flavoured deep-fried air. Coke is something made at the gasworks. Not to eat the last tiny scrap of school dinner had yet to be entered in The Book of Heavenly and Earthly Possibilities. Food left on plates was as unimaginable.

...but alas, the Worthless Rubbish Industry burgeons and School Cook, exhausted, gives in.

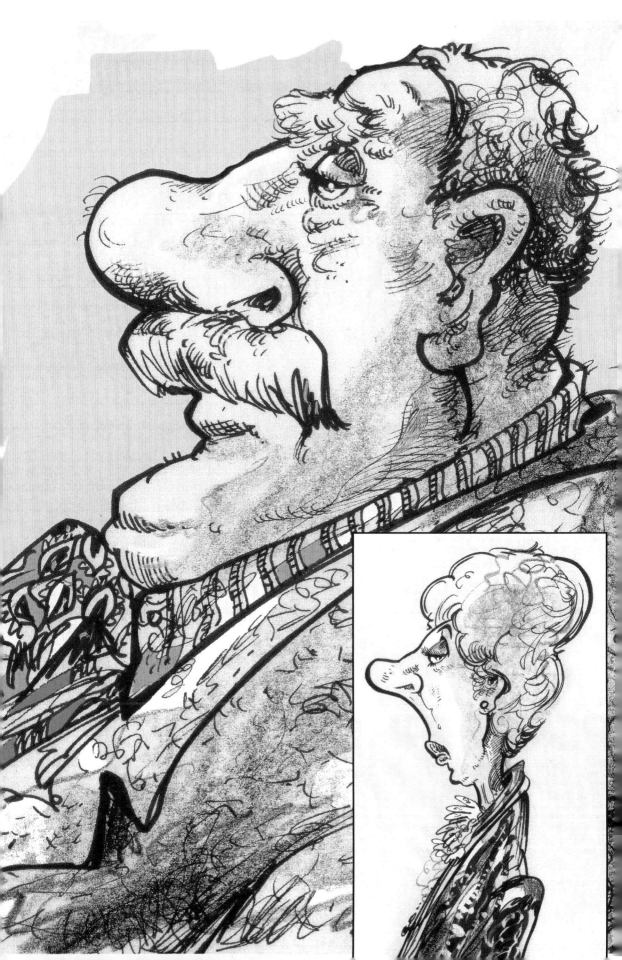

14TH BARONET AND LADY

Some phenomenally hardy pairs have survived but most exist only as deposits in the National Seedbank where, in desiccated form, they await The Last Trump.

Lady Marjorie swept into the panelled drawing room wearing the ermine-tipped Persian damask dressing gown which had been a present to her grandmother from the Akond of Swat.

"They are the fastest selling set of electric trains currently being sold" she declared, reading from a newspaper with one eye while the other searched the room for her half-empty glass of port and aquavit.

"What are, or is?" replied the 14th Baronet, Sir Fettes Hilary Tiverton-Dick of The Manor, rising to fetch himself a tin of Windbreaker, an Australian lager which their son Laddy, the Hon Galahad, was promoting at his PR agency, Dingle, Dangle, Bogamahony and Dick.

"With these incredible train sets" quoth Herself, "you can couple the cars or uncouple them, switch locomotive power on or off with easy finger action."

"Incredible indeed" said Sir Fettes. "What are you reading?"

"An advertisement. Listen. You also get a dual position lever switch."

"You mean a switch" said the noble lord.

"No, clodpoll. A dual position lever switch" thundered Lady Marjorie.

"You know, my dear" said Sir Fettes. "There's a board outside the Black Swan. It says 'Fayre Food'. F-A-Y kind of fare. Fayre Food. Hm? What what?"

"And the total track area circumscribes an impressive 1500 square centimetres in area." Lady Marjorie dropped the paper on her husband's lap on her way to the cellar in search of a bottle of Taylor's 1968 to go with the last of her Hrothgarsson Export Aquavit.

"Well, I never did" exclaimed the 14th B to himself, wondering how an area could circumscribe an area and how impressive, or sindeed what, 1500 square centimetres might be. Looking at the advert, he realised that for a few extra pounds he could have a 50-piece Farm Set to go with his train, including cows, sheep, geese, pigs, a farmer and two daughters.

Lady Marjorie, glass replenished, sat emphatically in the other leather armchair beside the fire and picked up the parish magazine, wondering what their lunatic vicar had written this month. Last time he had led with a metaphysical treatise on trying to reach God by combining prayer with the world wide web, blithering idiot.

Unnerved, Sir Fettes pressed half a dozen buttons at random on the little black thingery to do with the television receiver. An advertisement appeared for a herbal tonic. The voice told him that nothing was more complete. "Good Lord above, I pray you, let me have nothing, for apparently it is more complete. Marjorie?

I'm taking the dog out."

FARMER

Once the most common of all, Farmer is failing fast and is not expected to recover.

Mature Farmer has clearly identifiable markings of sticky-out ears, weatherbeaten skin, scrawny neck and a few wispy hairs beneath a flat tweed cap. The baldness and the ears have evolved through centuries of habitual behaviour. When told the price of anything, Farmer places one hand cupped behind an ear and with the other raises the cap slightly by the peak and scratches the top of his head, uttering the cry
"HOW much? ****ing hell!"

His reputation for parsimony far outstrips that of any other species. Your correspondent once had to telephone a neighbour, an East Anglian farmer, late in the evening. The following conversation ensued.

Your C: Sorry, John, to ring you so late. I've got some red bullocks in my garden. Do you know whose they are? Church Farm, right. Thanks. Anyway, you took a long time answering. I thought you had a phone by the bed.

Farmer: In the bedroom. I have to get out of bed to answer it.

Your C: Get out of bed? Why?

Farmer: Well, this chap gave me a phone, and I found a nice bit of wire in the barn, but it only reaches to the window sill.

Let the scene change to a builders' merchant's in rural Westmorland, whence your correspondent had removed. He observed a farmer of his acquaintance buying a cast-iron riddler for the Rayburn.

Your C: Hello, Mike. What are you doing buying new? Won't it weld?

Farmer: Aye, well, ah's welded it three times and it wain't weld ne' mair.

The Singing Postman, Alan Smethurst, had a song called 'You'll never see a farmer on a bike'. He was in fact referring to the evolved sub-variety Agribusinessman, then populous, now also reducing in numbers but increasing in size. Meanwhile, ravaged by epidemics, crucified by falling prices and tangled deep in impenetrable bureaucracy Farmer, for all the hardiness and pedigree going back to the beginnings of civilisation, is in especially rapid decline in upland regions. Travel to the Pennines, the Lakes, the Peak District, the Welsh hills You will see how poor Farmer is. All the members of the species have to share the same little black and white dog.

SCHOOLMISTRESS/HEADMISTRESS

Again dealing only with the state education system, Headmistress is almost certainly extinct, along with her neotic* form, Schoolmistress (*neoteny – physical maturity while still a juvenile, for example axolotl:salamander).

Schoolmistress wore a tweed suit, brogues, woollen stockings and had a huge bosom covered in pastel cashmere and decorated with a string of pearls. Her suit jacket had a diamante brooch in the lapel, or sometimes the enamel badge of the Soroptimists.

　　Most other points about Schoolmaster (*qv*) apply except that Schoolmistress never married. If the urge to mate transfixed her in her youth, it was always snuffed out by the tragic early death of her putative spouse in the war, or his running off with that brassy blonde who worked in Freeman, Hardy and Willis. Here, then, we have another example of a variety like Proper Doctor and Goat Woman which reliably appeared, but spontaneously, without line of descent. Remove the circumstances - no general war in which beloveds might die, no Freeman, Hardy and Willis - and there is nowhere to thrive and, indeed, no reason for existence.

　　If Schoolmistress developed into Headmistress, she would appear hardly changed except for the Presidency of the local branch of the British Council. As with Newspaper Seller, anyone sighting Schoolmistress should report the details immediately to the Natural History Museum.

SPY

*Spy is invisible and so it's very hard to know what one looks like
and, therefore, if it exists.*

We are quite sure that Spy as portrayed in the black and white films no longer exists. But, the state of the world tells us, the beautiful woman with the red lips, beveiled little hat and cigarette holder, and that man with the trench coat and trilby must have evolved or been replaced.

We can speculate that Spy has come in from the cold and sits in a secret office, staring at and listening to transmissions and emissions whereas before he and she were sent only on missions. But can the creature which searches electronically for the hidden truth be the same as the one played by Joseph Cotton in 'The Third Man' or Michael Caine in The Ipcress File'? Can anyone envisage such chaps searching the net for Arabic bloggers through the early hours, when they could be out drinking and chatting up birds in an ill-lit bar? Even if you could imagine such a thing, try Garbo as Mata Hari listening to Radio Peshawar and noting the odd inflection on the word for iron railings.

Identification of male Spy must have been fairly easy at one time. You just had to find a Leslie Howard lookalike having a coffee and reading the classified ads. He'd be searching for one which would trigger his actions, a message which he alone would understand as a call to arms. It could have been something mundane, like *The eagle has landed* or *The red dragons are flying tonight*. Others took a couple of nouns which didn't collocate and incorporated them into a sentence such as *The baguettes sleep in the tram, The madonna hates the white elephant stall, The monumental mason is a Jerusalem artichoke.*

Still others took a well known phrase or saying and altered it slightly: *Please put a pony in the old man's hat; A mouse lived in a wind tunnel in old Amsterdam; Life is just a bowl of curries.* All you would have had to do was buy a copy of the same paper and if you found one of those ads you had sighted Spy.

Nowadays, well, it could be anybody.

EPILOGUE FOR THE COMMON PEOPLE

The spaceman regenerated his appearance to conform with that of the local population, went for a walk and found himself thinking of home. It would be a Spring morning now, on the farm. His elder brother would have finished milking. He'd be sitting in the kitchen having bacon, eggs and fried bread with the paper propped up against the teapot. Mother would be fussing about trying to get the two youngest ready and on their bicycles in time for school.

Here where the spaceman stood it was Winter, a late afternoon in a strange population centre. Raindrops sparkled as they fell through the flickering light of what seemed to be methane gas lamps.

He sighed. What was he doing in Halifax anyway? Why did the government of his planet want to know what went on in this quark-forsaken hole in the earthyear of 2031? He looked at the placard outside the newsagents. *Smoke Ring Blown. Bacco users stubbed out in dragnet.*

He tuned his communicator to the local radio station. "A woman has been found guilty of wearing Eau de Cologne. She asked for six similar charges of endangering public health to be taken into consideration. A massive scare ensued at the airport this morning when customs officers discovered a whole salami sausage in a luggage bay. It was safely detonated later."

Across the way was a large stone building in classical style. The words Public Library were carved above the massive pillared doorway but a banner proclaimed it to be the People's Zoological Gardens. Seeking for further amusement, he paid and went into the zoo expecting lions and tigers and camels. Instead, he saw a few listless cows, ragged chickens, downhearted sheep and a very depressed pig. In need of cheering refreshment he went to the cafe. Behind the counter stood a large, red faced man wearing cord trousers, heavy boots, a cardigan over his plaid shirt and an old wax jacket.

"Steak, chips and a pint of old ale, please" said the spaceman.

"Nay, lad, you'll get me shot" said the earthling. "The sandwiches today are beancurd and lettuce, mushroom and curly kale, and dandelion and burdock. Juice is melon cauliflower. You're not from round here, are you?"

"Where I come from, we have steak, chips and old ale."

"What? With alcohol in it?" The spaceman nodded. "And I don't suppose you have black pudding, and cakes made with butter and sugar?" The spaceman nodded again, for thus it was. "And...and...I don't suppose you're allowed to go fishing, are you?"

"Indeed yes. And I regularly go and shoot rabbits for the pot."

The earthling looked inexpressibly glum. "Bless my aunt Fanny" he said. "By eckers, like". He bit into an endive and artichoke on granary. "Cakes and ale" he murmured. "Cakes and ale. Well. I'll go to the foot of our stairs".

Printed in Great Britain
by Amazon

19713386R00041